THE CIRCULATORY SYSTEM

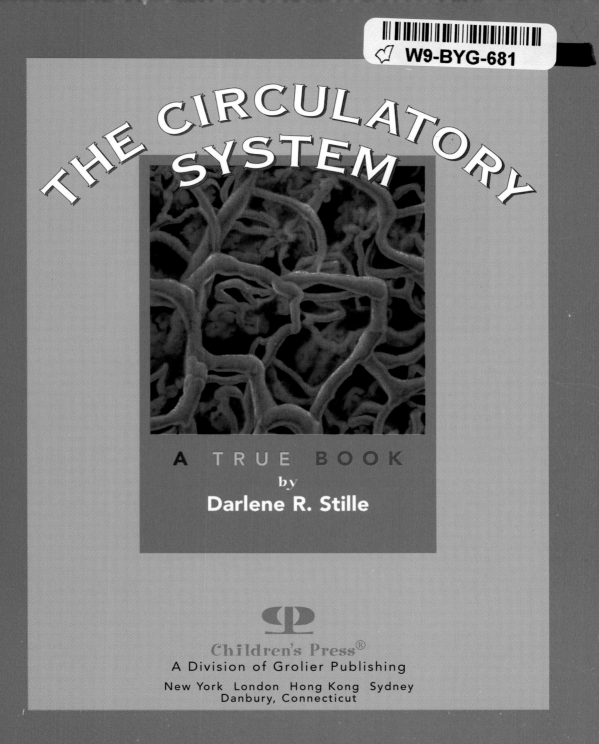

A TRUE BOOK

by

Darlene R. Stille

Children's Press®
A Division of Grolier Publishing
New York London Hong Kong Sydney
Danbury, Connecticut

Reading Consultant
Linda Cornwell
Learning Resource Consultant
Indiana Department of Education

Science Consultant
Ronald W. Schwizer, Ph.D.
Science Chair
Poly Prep Country Day School
Brooklyn, New York

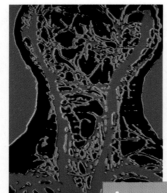

A special photograph showing arteries and veins of the head and neck

Library of Congress Cataloging-in-Publication Data

Stille, Darlene R.
    The Circulatory System / by Darlene R. Stille.
        p.   cm. — (A true book)
    Includes bibliographical references and index.
    Summary: Describes the various parts of the human circulatory system
and explains how and why blood is circulated throughout the body.
    ISBN 0-516-20438-6 (lib. bdg.)   0-516-26261-0 (pbk.)
    1. Cardiovascular system—Juvenile literature. 2. Blood-Circulation—
Juvenile literature. [1. Circulatory system. 2. Blood—Circulation.] I. Title.
II. Series.
QP111.6.S75   1997
612.1—dc21   96-2974
                                                                                                      CIP
                                                                                                       AC

Contents

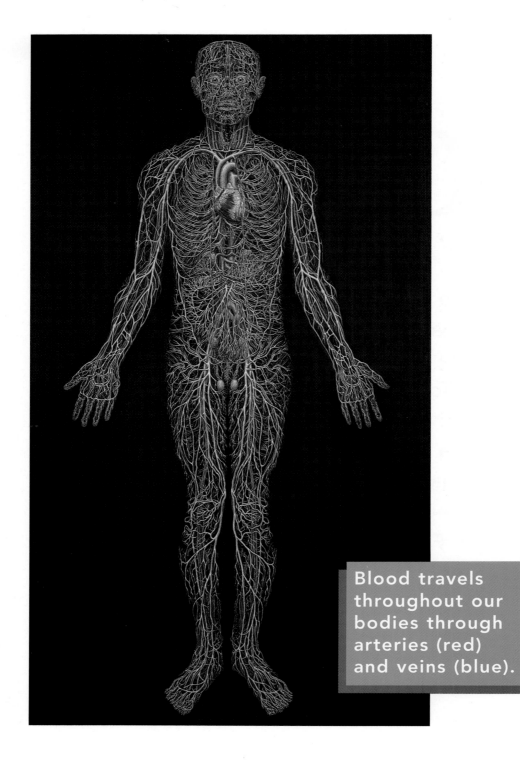

Blood travels throughout our bodies through arteries (red) and veins (blue).

The Heart and Blood Vessels

Blood keeps us alive. Blood goes everywhere in our bodies and carries everything our bodies need to live.

Blood travels through tubes in our bodies called blood vessels. Some blood vessels are big and some are very small.

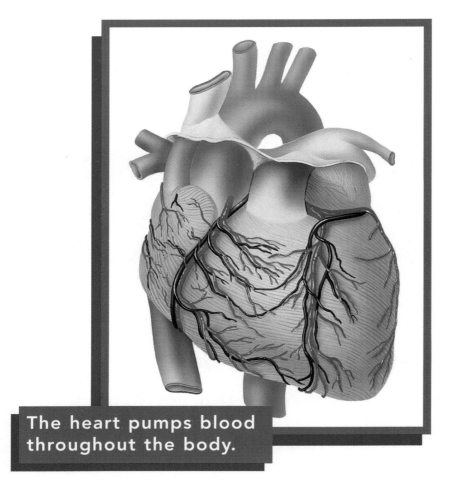

The heart pumps blood throughout the body.

Blood can move through these tubes because the heart pumps the blood to every part of the body. The sound of the heart pumping is called the heartbeat. Running makes the heart beat fast. You can feel your heart beating when you run.

When you run, your heart beats fast to bring more oxygen to your body.

The Heart Is a Pump

A pump pushes liquid or air through a tube or pipe. The heart is a pump that pushes blood through blood vessels.

The heart has four parts called chambers. The chambers hold blood that is entering or leaving the heart. The two top chambers hold blood

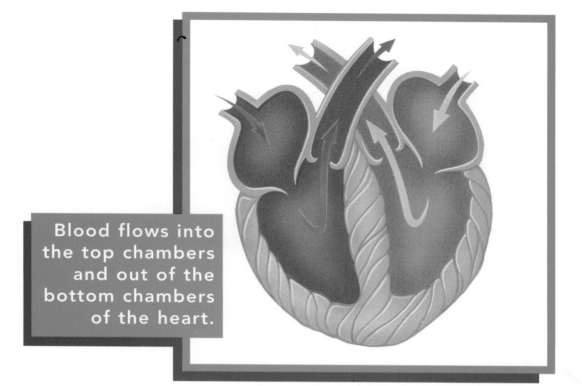

Blood flows into the top chambers and out of the bottom chambers of the heart.

coming into the heart. The two bottom chambers hold blood going out of the heart. Valves open and close to let blood in and out of these chambers.

The Heart Is a Muscle

Most pumps are made of metal, but the heart is made of muscle. The heart pumps when the heart muscle tightens.

Your heart is about the size of your fist. You can see what happens when muscles tighten if you make a fist. Notice how the muscles in your hand tighten.

When the heart pumps blood out to the body, it tightens like a fist.

This is how the heart muscle works. When the heart muscle tightens, blood goes out of the chambers.

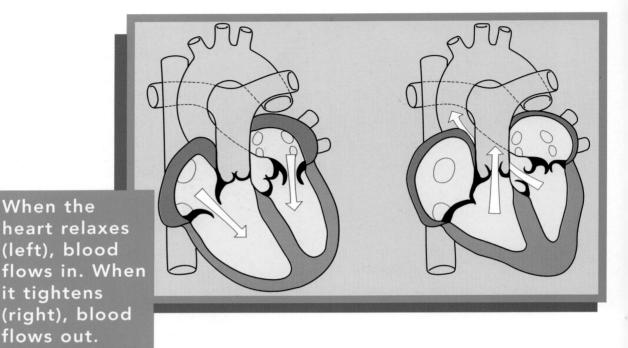

When the heart relaxes (left), blood flows in. When it tightens (right), blood flows out.

When the heart muscle relaxes, blood flows in.

But we do not have to think about our heart muscle to make it work. It tightens and relaxes all by itself.

What the Blood Does

Blood carries oxygen from the lungs to all the cells in the body. Blood also carries food to the cells. It picks up food from the intestines. Cells use oxygen and food to make energy. This energy keeps us alive.

When they make energy, the body's cells give off different

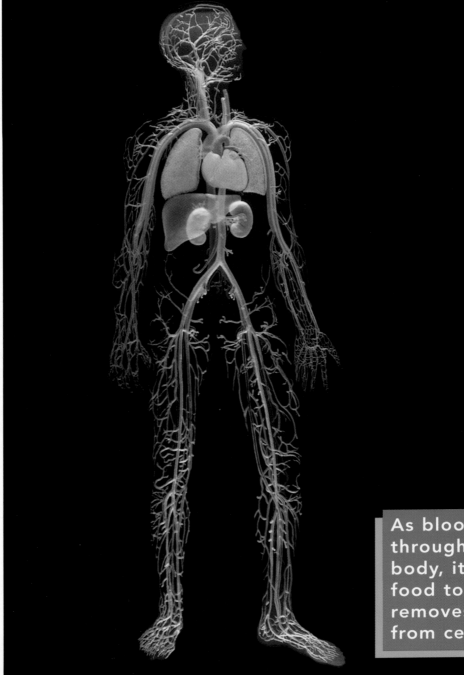

As blood travels through the body, it brings food to cells and removes waste from cells.

kinds of waste products, including a gas called carbon dioxide. Blood carries carbon dioxide away from the cells to the lungs so that we can breathe it out. Blood carries other waste products to the liver and the kidneys. This waste leaves the body as urine.

The heart and blood vessels are the body's highway system. This system carries the supplies that keep us alive and healthy.

The Heart and Lungs Work Together

When we breathe in, our lungs take in oxygen. The oxygen passes into our blood through blood vessels in the lungs. Blood with fresh oxygen then travels from the lungs to the heart.

This blood flows into the top left chamber of the

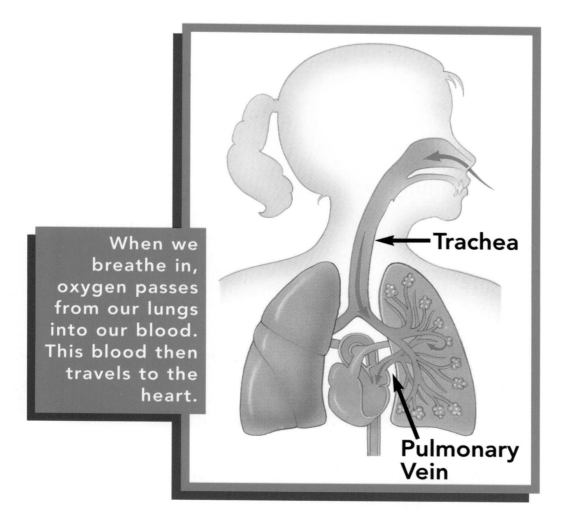

When we breathe in, oxygen passes from our lungs into our blood. This blood then travels to the heart.

Trachea

Pulmonary Vein

heart, called the left atrium. When this chamber is full, a valve opens. The blood flows through the valve into the

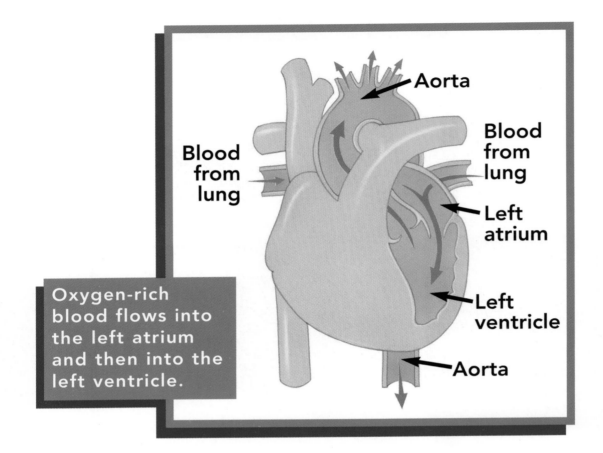

Aorta

Blood from lung

Blood from lung

Left atrium

Left ventricle

Aorta

Oxygen-rich blood flows into the left atrium and then into the left ventricle.

bottom left chamber—the left ventricle. The heart pumps the blood out of the left ventricle and into a large blood vessel called the aorta.

The Arteries

The aorta is an artery. Arteries are blood vessels that carry blood away from the heart. Arteries take oxygen-rich blood to all parts of the body, from the head to the toes.

The aorta is the largest artery in the body. Other large arteries branch off from

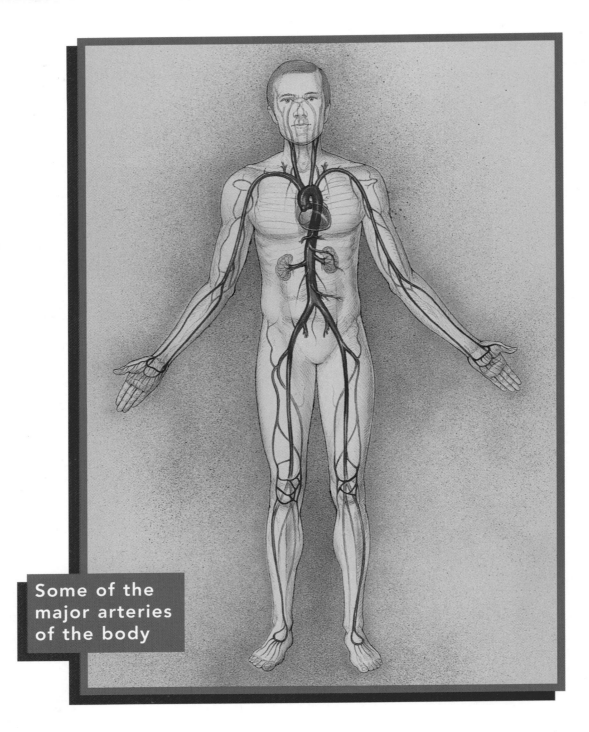

Some of the major arteries of the body

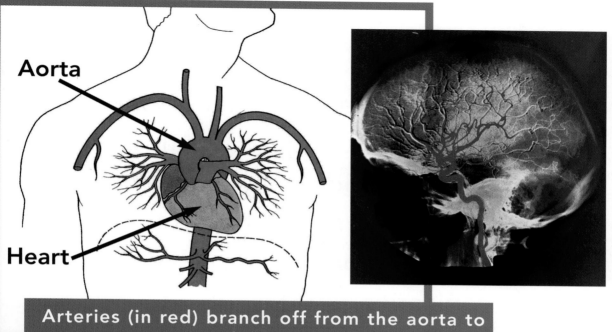

Aorta

Heart

Arteries (in red) branch off from the aorta to carry oxygen-rich blood to the rest of the body (left). A special X-ray (right) shows the arteries that supply blood to the brain.

the aorta. Some carry blood to the heart muscle and the brain. Others carry blood to the arms and legs or to the abdomen and chest.

Smaller and smaller arteries keep branching off like tiny rivers. Blood finally reaches the body's cells through the tiniest blood vessels, called capillaries.

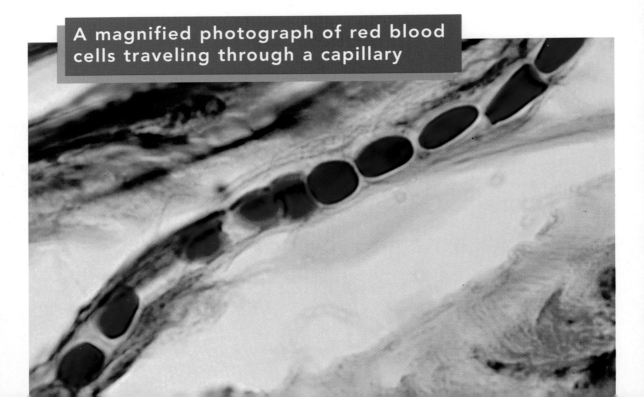

A magnified photograph of red blood cells traveling through a capillary

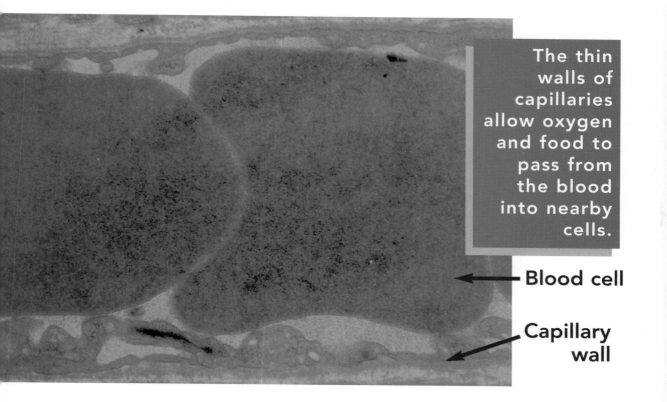

The thin walls of capillaries allow oxygen and food to pass from the blood into nearby cells.

Blood cell

Capillary wall

At the cells, the blood drops off oxygen and picks up the waste product carbon dioxide. Then the blood starts its return trip to the heart through the veins.

The Veins

Veins are blood vessels that carry blood back to the heart. At the cells, tiny capillaries carry the carbon-dioxide-rich blood to small veins. Throughout the body, small veins lead into larger veins. For example, small veins in the hands and feet flow into larger veins in the arms and legs.

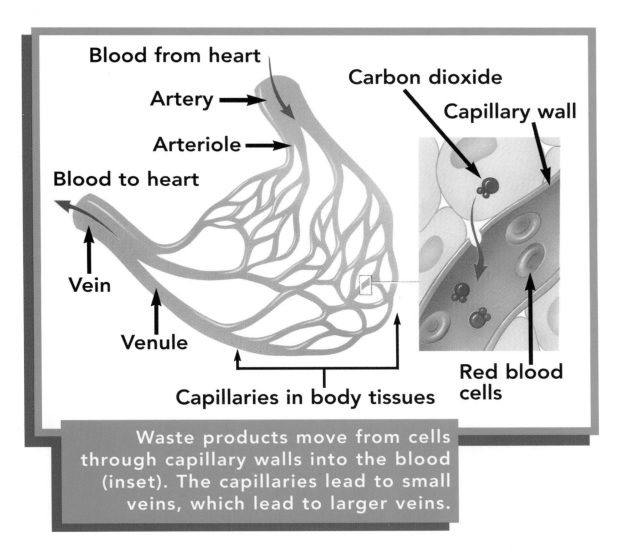

Blood from heart

Artery →

Arteriole →

Blood to heart

Vein

Venule

Carbon dioxide

Capillary wall

Red blood cells

Capillaries in body tissues

Waste products move from cells through capillary walls into the blood (inset). The capillaries lead to small veins, which lead to larger veins.

Finally, all the blood flows into two main veins. One vein collects blood coming back

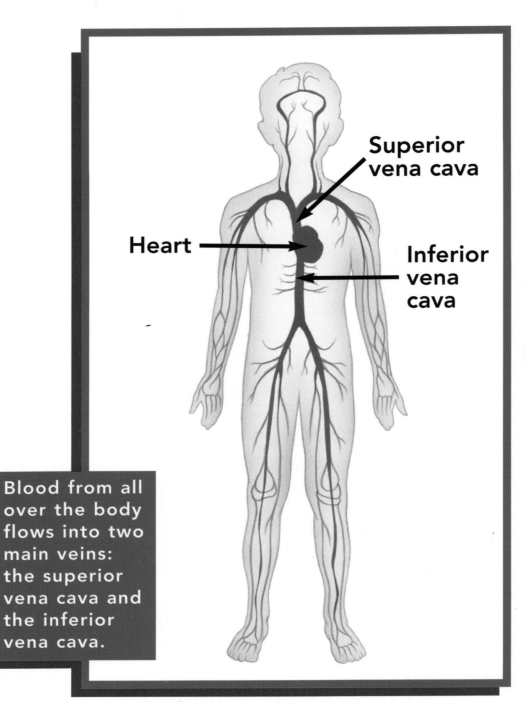

Superior vena cava

Heart

Inferior vena cava

Blood from all over the body flows into two main veins: the superior vena cava and the inferior vena cava.

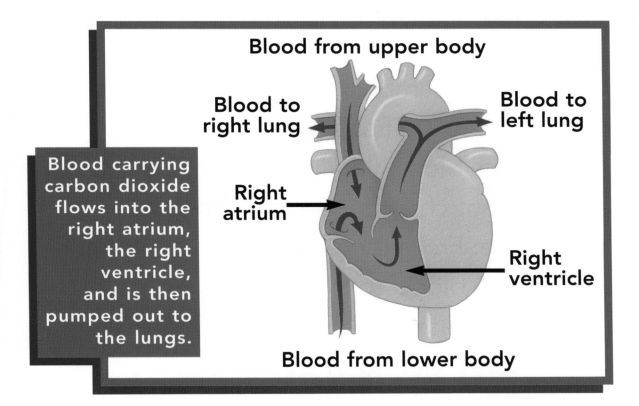

Blood from upper body

Blood to right lung

Blood to left lung

Blood carrying carbon dioxide flows into the right atrium, the right ventricle, and is then pumped out to the lungs.

Right atrium

Right ventricle

Blood from lower body

from the head and arms. The other collects blood from the legs, abdomen, and chest.

These two main veins deliver the blood to the heart. Both veins connect to the top chamber on the right side of the heart. When this chamber (called the right atrium) is full, a valve opens. This lets blood flow into the bottom right chamber—the right ventricle. From there, the heart pumps the blood to the lungs.

When you breathe out, your lungs get rid of carbon dioxide in your blood.

When you breathe in, the blood in your lungs receives a fresh supply of oxygen. This blood then flows back to the heart, and the whole process starts over again.

What Causes a Heart Attack

To keep our bodies healthy, the heart and blood vessels must work properly. The heart muscle must be strong, and the coronary arteries that carry food and oxygen to the heart muscle must be clean and open.

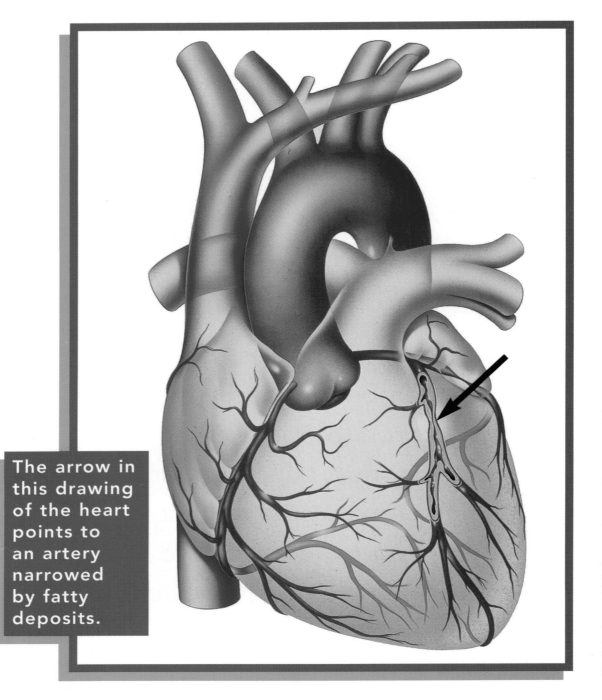

The arrow in this drawing of the heart points to an artery narrowed by fatty deposits.

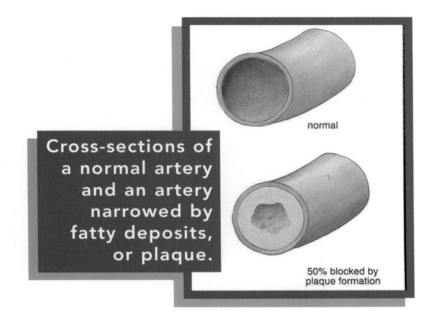

Cross-sections of a normal artery and an artery narrowed by fatty deposits, or plaque.

normal

50% blocked by plaque formation

But fatty deposits can make the inside of these blood vessels narrow. If a coronary artery becomes blocked, blood cannot flow to the heart. If blood does not reach the heart, the heart muscle starts to die. When this happens, a person suffers a heart attack.

Doctors can help some people with blocked arteries. The doctor might give them drugs or insert a tube with a tiny balloon into the blocked artery. Then the doctor inflates the balloon to push the fatty deposit away. This procedure is called an angioplasty.

These X rays show an artery before (above) and after (right) angioplasty.

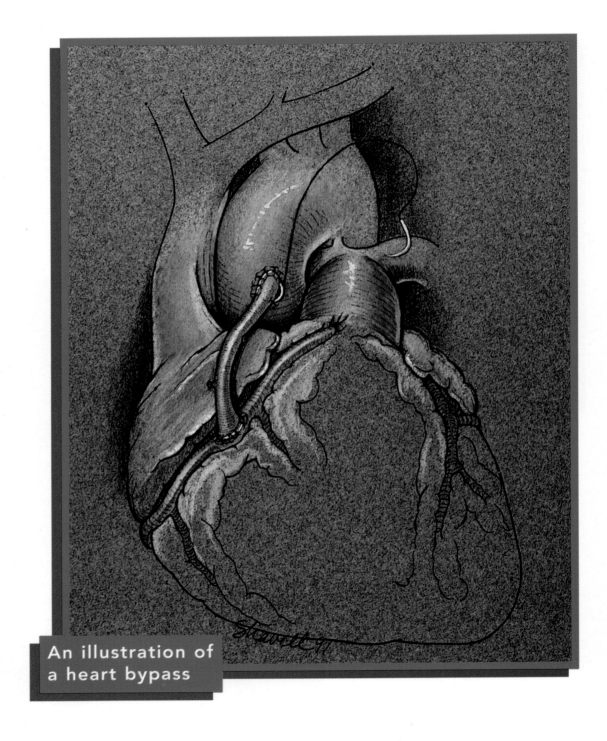

An illustration of
a heart bypass

In very serious cases, the doctor may order bypass surgery. The surgeon sews a blood vessel from another part of the body to the coronary arteries. This new blood vessel carries blood around the blocked artery.

If the heart muscle is too damaged to be repaired, the doctor might call for a heart transplant. A new human heart is used to replace the sick heart. The heart used in the

A human
heart ready
for transplant

transplant is usually taken from
another human who has died
in an accident. Heart surgery is
very serious. So it is best to
keep your heart healthy.

Artificial Hearts

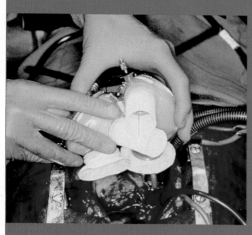

Heart transplants are hard to get. People who need them must wait a long time, and some people die before a heart is available. So, surgeons have experimented with putting artificial hearts in patients until a real heart becomes available. Scientists are trying to develop artificial hearts that work as well as human hearts.

Keeping Your Heart Healthy

There are simple things you can do to keep your heart healthy. The heart is a muscle, and muscles get stronger when they are exercised. So exercise can help keep your heart healthy.

Exercise
keeps your
heart healthy.

Eating healthy foods can help keep fatty deposits from forming in your heart and arteries.

Any exercise that makes the heart beat fast will help keep your heart healthy. Running, swimming, and bicycling can make the heart beat fast. Even fast walking will make the heart beat fast and help your heart muscle stay strong.

Eating the right foods is also important for your heart. Fatty foods are bad for your heart because they help create the fatty deposits that block blood vessels.

Fruits and vegetables are good for your heart because they help keep fatty deposits from forming. Whole-grain breads and cereals are also good for your heart.

Snacks high in salt are bad for your heart—and so is smoking. Smoking is a major cause of heart disease. Not smoking cigarettes is one of the best things you can do for your heart.

Swimming is a good way to keep your heart healthy.

Your heart needs to beat for the rest of your life. So it is never too early to start helping your heart do its job.

To Find Out More

Here are some additional resources to help you learn more about the circulatory system:

 **Books**

Bryan, Jenny. **Body Talk: The Pulse of Life.** Dillon Press, 1993.

Cole, Joanna. **The Magic School Bus: Inside the Human Body.** Scholastic, Inc., 1989.

Parker, Steve. **The Heart and Blood.** Franklin Watts, 1989.

Showers, Paul. **A Drop of Blood.** Thomas Y. Crowell, 1989.

American Heart Association
7272 Greenville Avenue
Dallas, TX 75231
214-373-6300
http:/www.amhrt.org/index.html

Learn how the heart works, along with arteries, veins, and the blood. Also find news and information about the AHA and its services.

ExploraNet
http://www. exploratorium.edu/

Visit a constantly changing assortment of online exhibits presented by the Exploratorium.

The Exploratorium
3601 Lyon Street
San Francisco, CA 94123
415-563-7337
415-563-0307 (fax)

The Franklin Institute Science Museum
222 North 20th Street
Philadelphia, PA 19103
215-448-1200

Museum of Health and Medical Science
1515 Hermann Drive
Houston, TX 77004
713-521-1515
http://www.mhms.org/enter.html

Visit the "Amazing Body Pavilion" to explore the heart, lungs, digestive system, and more.

Museum of Science and Industry
57th Street & Lake Shore Dr.
Chicago, IL
773-684-1414

National Heart, Lung, and Blood Institute
P.O. Box 30105
Bethesda, MD 20824-0105
301-251-1223 (fax)

Important Words

abdomen the part of the human body between the chest and the hips

aorta largest artery in the body

arteries blood vessels that carry blood away from the heart to every part of the body

blood vessels tubes that carry blood through the body

capillaries tiniest blood vessels in the body

carbon dioxide gas that our cells give off as a waste product

oxygen gas in our air that we need to breathe in order to live; our body's cells use it to make energy

valve in the heart and veins, a fold of tissue that that allows blood to flow in only one direction

veins blood vessels that carry blood back to the heart from everywhere in the body

Index

Meet the Author

Darlene Stille lives in Chicago and is executive editor of the World Book Annuals and World Book's Online Service. She has written several Children's Press books, including *Extraordinary Women Scientists, Extraordinary Women of Medicine,* and three other True Books on the body systems.

The photograph on the title page shows a capillary network magnified many times.